# HANDY HEALTH GUIDE TO ADHD

Alvin and Virginia Silverstein
and Laura Silverstein Nunn

 **Enslow Publishers, Inc.**
40 Industrial Road
Box 398
Berkeley Heights, NJ 07922
USA

http://www.enslow.com

Original edition published as *Attention Deficit Disorder* in 2001.

**Library of Congress Cataloging-in-Publication Data**

Silverstein, Alvin.
Handy health guide to ADHD / by Alvin Silverstein, Virginia Silverstein and Laura Silverstein Nunn.
    p. cm. — (Handy health guides)
  Summary: "An overview of ADHD for children in grades 5 and up. Find out what ADHD is, how it is diagnosed, and some treatment options"— Provided by publisher.
Includes index.
  ISBN 978-0-7660-4270-4
  1. Attention-deficit hyperactivity disorder—Juvenile literature.  I. Silverstein, Virginia B. II. Nunn, Laura Silverstein. III. Title.
  RJ506.H9S562 2013
  618.92'8589—dc23

                        2012028925


Future editions:
Paperback ISBN: 978-1-4644-0483-2
EPUB ISBN: 978-1-4645-1250-6
Single-User PDF ISBN: 978-1-4646-1250-3
Multi-UserPDF ISBN: 978-0-7660-5882-8

Printed in the United States of America

052013 Lake Book Manufacturing, Inc., Melrose Park, IL

10 9 8 7 6 5 4 3 2 1

**To Our Readers:** We have done our best to make sure all Internet Addresses in this book were active and appropriate when we went to press. However, the author and the publisher have no control over and assume no liability for the material available on those Internet sites or on other Web sites they may link to. Any comments or suggestions can be sent by e-mail to comments@enslow.com or to the address on the back cover.

♻ Enslow Publishers, Inc., is committed to printing our books on recycled paper. The paper in every book contains 10% to 30% post-consumer waste (PCW). The cover board on the outside of each book contains 100% PCW. Our goal is to do our part to help young people and the environment too!

**Illustration Credits:** AP Images/Jeff Chiu, p. 14; Joseph Abbott/Photos.com, p. 29; Jupiterimages/Photos.com, p. 11; mocker_bat/Photos.com, p. 42; s_bukley/Shutterstock.com, p. 9; Shutterstock.com, pp. 1, 3, 4, 6, 10, 13, 16, 17, 18, 19, 20, 22, 23, 24, 27, 28, 32, 33, 38, 41; Sponge/Wikipedia, p. 35; Tim Sharville/Photos.com, p. 39.

**Cover Photo:** Shutterstock.com (all images)

# CONTENTS

All teens love to run around and have fun. It's a natural part of being young.

# 1

# OUT OF CONTROL

Are you full of energy and always on the go? Do you have problems sitting still? When you want something, do you have to have it *right now*? Do you call out answers in class and never wait your turn?

Do have trouble finishing your homework or chores because you are easily distracted? Does your mind constantly switch from one idea to another? Is it hard to focus for long on just one thing?

If this describes you or somebody you know, you or your friend might have attention deficit hyperactivity disorder. Or you might not. After all, most children are full of energy and easily distracted. They often act on impulse, without thinking. So sometimes it's hard to tell whether a child really has attention deficit hyperactivity disorder, or ADHD for short.

## Hyperactive!

ADHD used to be called hyperactivity, because a telltale sign of the condition is being overactive. The word *hyper* means "too much." A hyperactive person is a lot more active than most people. He or she usually has trouble sitting still. Hyperactive teens often fidget, rock back and forth, or suddenly jump up and run around.

ADHD is a real problem that affects millions of children, teenagers, and adults. Some doctors consider ADHD a disease, like asthma. But ADHD symptoms come out in behavior, not something physical like coughing and wheezing.

People usually picture hyperactive kids when they think of ADHD. But some kids with ADHD are not hyperactive at all. They tend to be quiet and dreamy. Instead of paying attention to what is going on around them, they get lost in their own daydreams. They do not cause the same kind of problems at home and in school that hyperactive kids do, but they have problems of their own. They can't concentrate, so they have trouble learning new things.

Kids with ADHD, whether they are hyperactive or calm, have a hard time controlling their behavior. They usually do not know when they are getting out of control so they may have trouble learning in school, behaving at home, or making and keeping friends.

If you or someone you know has ADHD, there are things you can do. Some treatments can help, and kids with ADHD can learn to control their behavior better.

# 2

# WHO GETS ADHD?

For many years, scientists believed that only kids get attention deficit hyperactivity disorder. They thought that kids just "grow out of it" before they become adults. Studies have shown that this is not always true. About 3 to 8 percent of kids in the United States have attention deficit hyperactivity disorder. More than half of these children will continue to have ADHD symptoms when they grow up.

Adults with ADHD are not usually hyperactive. That may be why doctors used to think that kids grow out of it. Adults with ADHD often have trouble paying attention and may act quickly, without thinking. They may also have trouble with relationships and have a hard time finishing projects. Some may not be able to keep a job for very long. This can really hurt their self-confidence and self-esteem.

# Famous People With ADHD

Some historians and psychologists believe that a number of famous people—past and present—have had ADHD. The condition may not have been officially identified; their view is based on descriptions of the person's behavior.

| NAME | OCCUPATION |
|---|---|
| Ludwig van Beethoven | Composer |
| Jim Carrey | Actor/comedian |
| Albert Einstein | Physicist |
| Dwight D. Eisenhower | U.S. President |
| Howie Mandel | Comedian/TV host |
| Wolfgang Amadeus Mozart | Composer |
| Michael Phelps | Olympic athlete |
| Pablo Picasso | Artist |
| Will Smith | Actor/rapper |
| Justin Timberlake | Actor/singer |

9

Children as young as three years old may show signs of ADHD. But their parents may think they just have a lot of energy. The symptoms are more likely to be noticed around school age, when kids are expected to learn to follow rules and control their behavior.

People with ADHD often have family members—parents, grandparents, aunts, uncles, brothers or sisters, or cousins—who also have ADHD. If one identical twin has ADHD, the other twin is very likely to have it too.

**Kids who can't learn to control their behavior in school may be very distracting to their classmates.**

# 3

# WHAT'S ADHD ALL ABOUT?

A person with attention deficit hyperactivity disorder has trouble controlling his or her behavior in different settings, such as home or school. Not all kids with ADHD behave in the same way, however. In fact, ADHD symptoms can vary a great deal.

Some kids with ADHD are full of energy and can't sit still. Others are calm, but can't concentrate and have trouble paying attention. That's why doctors often talk about three types of ADHD: inattentive type, hyperactive-impulsive type, and combined type.

**Acting out of control can be a sign of ADHD.**

## ADD or ADHD?

You may have heard people talking about ADD (attention deficit disorder). Many doctors do not use this term anymore. They prefer to call it attention deficit hyperactivity disorder or ADHD because they believe this name is a better way of describing the different forms this condition may take.

Kids with the inattentive type have trouble paying attention. This type is often called ADD—attention deficit disorder—because hyperactivity is not a problem here. Instead, they may have trouble learning in class because they are too busy daydreaming. Their minds are often filled with so many thoughts and ideas that it's hard to concentrate on only one thing. Because these children have a hard time focusing, they often make careless mistakes and have trouble finishing projects. They also find it hard to keep track of things and become distracted easily.

Kids with the hyperactive-impulsive type of ADHD are full of energy and always on the go. Hyperactive kids are often fidgety and squirm in their seats. They may

Having lots of energy and always being on the go can be signs of the hyperactive-impulsive type of ADHD.

**College student Blake Taylor has been on medication since he was diagnosed with ADHD at the age of five.**

run around or jump and climb when they are supposed to be sitting still. They may talk constantly, too. Impulsive kids can't wait their turn. They often speak before they think, and they frequently interrupt other people.

## Activity 1:
## What's It Like to Have ADHD?

If you don't have ADHD, try to imagine what it feels like. First, turn on the TV and the radio. Then ask a friend to talk to you. While all this is going on, sit down and try to do your homework. Can you tune out all of the distractions and do your homework? Can you talk to your friend without paying attention to the TV or radio? Some people with ADHD have trouble focusing on just one thing at a time and tuning out the rest.

Some kids with ADHD have the combined type. They show both inattentive and hyperactive-impulsive symptoms. They are easily distracted and have trouble finishing projects. They are also fidgety and impulsive. Their behavior may change from day to day—they may be quiet and dreamy one day and bubbling over with energy the next.

It's not easy to deal with people who have ADHD. Can you imagine trying to talk to someone who acts like a space cadet and doesn't seem to listen to you?

Do you have a friend who can't wait for his or her turn when you're playing a game? Sometimes it seems like people with ADHD are unfriendly, too talkative, or mean. That's why some kids with ADHD have trouble making and keeping friends. They are often fun to be around because they have lots of imaginative

It's normal for friends to disagree. But some people have trouble spending lots of time with a friend who has ADHD if she is too talkative or sometimes hard to understand.

Everyone has disagreements once in a while, like this mom and her son. But kids with ADHD often have trouble getting along with their parents and siblings.

ideas and a great sense of humor. But it can be hard to spend lot of time with them.

Kids with ADHD may also have trouble getting along with their own family. They may not listen to their parents, or they may fight with their brothers and sisters all the time. Eventually, kids with ADHD may feel as though they can no longer relate to the people in their lives. This can make them feel sad and lonely. They don't feel good about themselves and they may develop low self-esteem.

# Superstars With ADHD

People who have ADHD may feel that they are bad, lazy, or stupid, but that's not true. Many people with ADHD are very smart and creative. In fact, most people with ADHD have average intelligence or higher.

You might be surprised to learn that people with ADHD have become teachers, doctors, lawyers, movie stars, company presidents, or athletes. Some of the most important and inventive people in history had ADHD. For example, some medical experts believe that Benjamin Franklin and Thomas Edison both might have had ADHD.

# 4
# WHAT CAUSES ADHD?

Scientists have learned a lot about ADHD in recent years. They now know that it is not caused by poor parenting or bad teachers. Many people think that eating a lot of sugar can make kids hyperactive. But scientists have learned that most cases of ADHD are not caused by a high-sugar diet. Most experts believe that ADHD occurs when part of a person's brain doesn't work quite right.

If you ate all this candy you might get hyper for a little while, but candy doesn't cause ADHD.

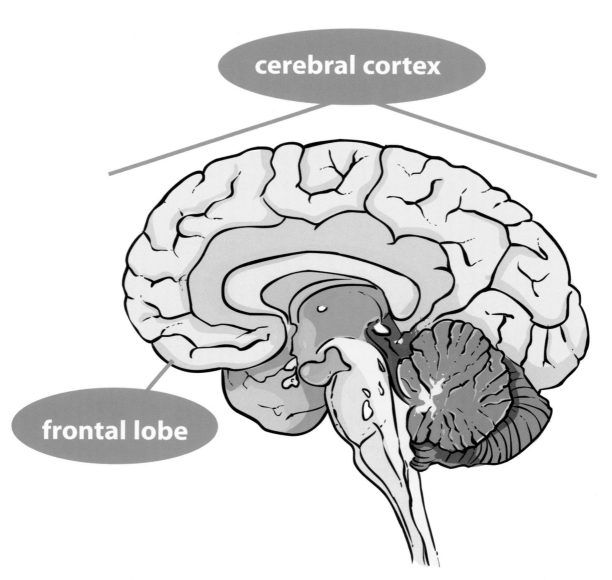

**cerebral cortex**

**frontal lobe**

The cerebral cortex is the outermost layer of your brain, while the frontal lobe is located right behind your forehead.

20

Each part of your brain has a special job to do. The outermost layer of your brain is called the cerebral cortex. You use it to think, remember, and make decisions. You also use it to understand and form words and to control body movements. The cerebral cortex receives messages from your ears, eyes, nose, taste buds, and skin, and lets you know what is going on in the world around you.

Deeper inside the brain there is a kind of relay station that contains billions of nerve cells. These nerve cells receive messages from different parts of the body and send out messages to control body activities. Chemicals called neurotransmitters help to carry these messages from one part of the brain to another. Whenever you concentrate on something—whether it's homework or playing catch with your friends— nerve cells fire off messages back and forth at very high speeds. This fast-paced action makes it possible for you to block out distractions and focus on what you are doing.

The part of the brain right behind your forehead is called the frontal lobe. It helps you pay attention, focus on one thing at a time, make plans and stick to them,

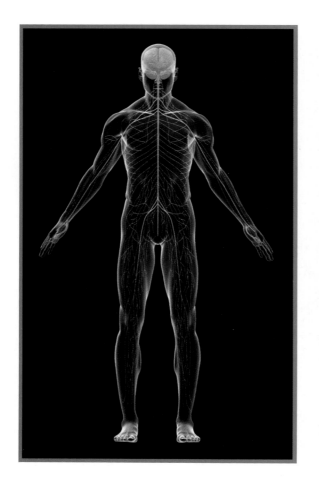 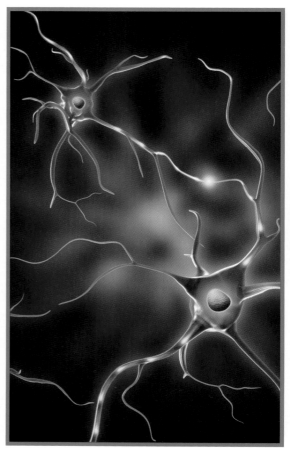

A network of nerves connects the brain and spinal cord with all parts of the body (left). The branches of a nerve cell (right) pick up messages from other nerve cells and send them on to the next nerve cell in the chain. Eventually, the message reaches the brain.

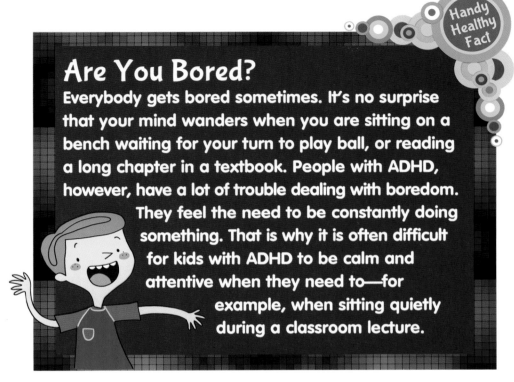

## Are You Bored?

Everybody gets bored sometimes. It's no surprise that your mind wanders when you are sitting on a bench waiting for your turn to play ball, or reading a long chapter in a textbook. People with ADHD, however, have a lot of trouble dealing with boredom. They feel the need to be constantly doing something. That is why it is often difficult for kids with ADHD to be calm and attentive when they need to—for example, when sitting quietly during a classroom lecture.

and think before you act. In many people with ADHD, some structures in the frontal lobe of the brain are smaller than usual. As a result, the nerve cells in this area can't pick up enough of an important neurotransmitter known as dopamine. At the same time, some nerve cells grab dopamine before it reaches the places where it is needed.

Dopamine helps a person block out distractions and control his or her behavior. When too little dopamine is moving through the brain, a person has trouble focusing

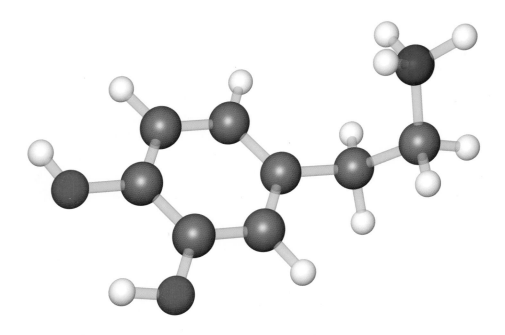

This model shows the chemical structure of dopamine, an important neurotransmitter.

on one thing. Some people may also have trouble controlling their actions. That's what happens to many people with ADHD.

ADHD is usually an inherited condition. People who have the condition were born with it. Some cases, however, have been linked to other possible causes. For example, a woman who drinks alcohol, smokes, or takes drugs while she is pregnant may damage the developing brain of her unborn child. But, most of the time, ADHD is passed along in the genes. Genes are chemicals that carry inherited traits. In people with ADHD, the genes that control the way the brain uses dopamine are different from the genes that most people have.

# 5

# DIAGNOSING ADHD

It's not easy to decide whether a child has ADHD. After all, most kids are restless at times. So how do you know whether someone has ADHD or is just an energetic person?

Unfortunately, there is no sure way to know because the symptoms of ADHD are similar to those of many other conditions.

For example, ear infections can affect a child's hearing and make it seem as though he or she is not listening. Allergies or seizures may also cause behaviors that seem like ADHD—so can family problems, a boring teacher, or a learning disability. A child who seems quiet and withdrawn may be suffering from depression rather than ADHD. With all these

Does this boy have ADHD
or just a lot of energy?

# A Learning Link

Many experts believe there is a strong link between ADHD and learning disabilities. As many as 50 percent of people with ADHD also have trouble with their schoolwork, especially reading and math. This can happen even when a person is really smart. Many people think that ADHD and learning disabilities are the same thing, but they are not! Sometimes it may be hard to tell the difference. It may seem like a child is not paying attention when the real problem is a learning disability. Similarly, children who have trouble focusing their attention may have trouble learning even though they do not have a learning disability.

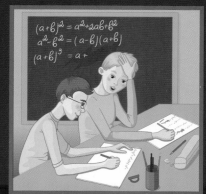

possibilities, deciding whether a child has ADHD can be tough. It's very important for doctors to get the diagnosis right because different problems need different treatments.

A physical exam is usually a good way to start making a diagnosis. It can rule out other medical problems. The doctor will also ask a lot of questions. Is there any history of medical problems? Does the person get along well with others? How does he behave

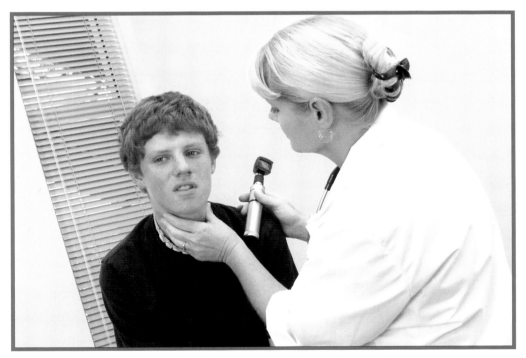

A physical exam can rule out other medical conditions.

at home and at school? How long has the person been behaving this way? How often is the behavior a problem?

If the doctor thinks the person may have ADHD, he or she may suggest that a school counselor see the student. The counselor will ask more questions, looking for examples of inattentive behavior and hyperactive or impulsive behavior. The counselor may also ask the student to take a few tests that can provide a better understanding of his problems.

Everybody fidgets or lacks focus from time to time. Doctors and counselors will decide that a child has ADHD only if he shows many of the behaviors listed in the chart on page 31. These behaviors must have continued for at least six months, and they must have appeared before the child was seven years old.

These behaviors are generally more serious in a child with ADHD, and they happen more often than in other children of the same age. Also, the behaviors create major problems in at least two areas of a child's life: school, home, or social settings with friends. If a child has problems at school but behaves normally at home and with friends, he probably does not have ADHD.

# Checklist for Diagnosing ADHD

**Inattentive Type:**

- often daydreams in class
- is easily distracted
- can't remember the teacher's instructions
- often loses or forgets homework or books
- makes careless mistakes in schoolwork
- doesn't listen to parents when asked to do a task
- doesn't stick with a task until it's done

**Hyperactive-Impulsive Type:**

- fidgets a lot and can't sit still
- blurts out answers in class
- interrupts friends while they are speaking
- can't wait for his or her turn in games or groups
- is always "on the go," running around a lot or climbing up on things when he or she is supposed to be sitting
- is full of ideas and talks constantly

Boys are three times more likely to be diagnosed with ADHD than girls. But that doesn't mean it is rare in girls. Boys tend to have the hyperactive-impulsive type. They get noticed because they are bursting with energy and often get into trouble at school. Girls, on the other hand, are more likely to have the inattentive type (ADD). They are likely to go unnoticed because they are low-key and quiet in class. If they are hyperactive, girls usually act in different ways than boys. For example, they may be very talkative, and people think they are "too chatty."

**Having problems learning in school could be a sign of ADHD.**

# How Common Is ADHD?

Would you believe that in the United States at least one child in a class of twenty-five to thirty kids is diagnosed with ADHD? This is hard to believe, which is why some people think that ADHD is being overdiagnosed. Medical experts disagree. They say that because scientists have learned a lot about ADHD in recent years, doctors are now better able to identify it.

# 6

# TREATING ADHD

When most people think about ADHD, they also think about Ritalin®. The medicine, Ritalin, is used to treat ADHD. Many people are frightened by the idea of giving kids a drug that they will take every day for many years. They also think that too many children are being treated with Ritalin. Others think of Ritalin as a "magic pill" that can make ADHD disappear. Ritalin can help kids with ADHD focus better and control their behavior, but it does not cure ADHD.

As many as 80 percent of children with ADHD are helped by Ritalin and other ADHD medications. These drugs are stimulants that usually make people feel more wide awake and full of energy. Some people with sleep problems take Ritalin to stay awake during the day.

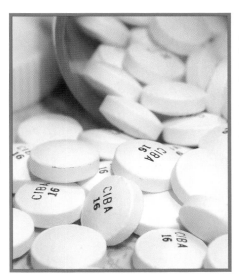

Many kids with ADHD need to take medication every single day.

Ritalin doesn't make kids with ADHD more hyper or active. Instead, it seems to calm them down. It helps them pay attention and concentrate so they are not as easily distracted. In children with ADHD, Ritalin brings chemicals in the brain back to levels that are normal.

ADHD medications are safe and effective when taken under a doctor's care. But they can have some annoying side effects, such as headaches, increased anxiety, stomachaches, and sleep problems. A high dose of the drug may cause more serious problems, such as an increased heart rate and blood pressure, mood changes, and confusion. Doctors usually start with the lowest dose and then raise it gradually until it is just right.

For treatment to be successful, children with ADHD need the support of their parents, teachers, and

## ADHD Patch

In 2006, the first skin patch became available to treat ADHD in children ages six to seventeen. The ADHD patch, called Daytrana®, is designed to be worn on the child's hip for up to nine hours. It releases the same stimulant that is in Ritalin. If there are any bad side effects, the patch can simply be removed.

counselors. Counselors can help children and family members learn about ADHD and how to deal with it. They can also talk to children about their problems and help them feel better about themselves. They can help reduce the child's worries and anxieties. They can also teach the child how to handle specific situations at home, at school, or with friends.

Parents and teachers need to learn about ADHD so they can understand what the child is going through. The more parents and teachers know about ADHD, the more they can help kids with these problems. This way, both parents and teachers can learn ways to change the behavior into something more acceptable.

Behavior modification is a technique often used to change a person's behavior. The parent, teacher, or counselor sets goals for a person with ADHD. They reward good behavior and either ignore bad behavior or work with the person to correct it. There are three steps in this process:

1. *Define the problem.* For example, does the person constantly have trouble sitting still? In this case the problem is restlessness.

2. *Set a reasonable goal.* The person might begin by trying to sit still during dinner. At first, it may be too hard for a person with ADHD to sit still until everyone has finished eating. It is a good idea to break up the big goal into little goals that are easier to reach. For instance, the person can try sitting at the table for five minutes, then ten minutes, then fifteen minutes.

3. *Work toward the goal.* Kids with ADHD respond well to rewards and consequences. Parents and teachers should praise the child whenever he makes some progress, even if the child does not

achieve the goal. This will show that they are proud of the child's progress. A parent might say, "I like how well you sat through dinner." One way to reward kids for good behavior is by planning a special reward, like lunch at a favorite restaurant.

If the person is working toward a goal, progress can be marked on a chart or spreadsheet. After the person collects a certain number of points, he will receive a reward, like a trip to the movies.

A reward, such as new music, is a great way to encourage continued success in ADHD management.

# ADHD Video Games

Many people say that kids today spend too much time playing computer games. That could explain why more and more kids are having a hard time staying focused on things away from the computer, such as in the classroom or sitting at the dinner table. Whether or not that is true, special computer game systems, such as one called Play Attention, have been designed to help children with ADHD to focus better. These games work to train the child's brain to pay attention. Many parents worry about the long-term effects of ADHD medications. These special video games give them a harmless alternative.

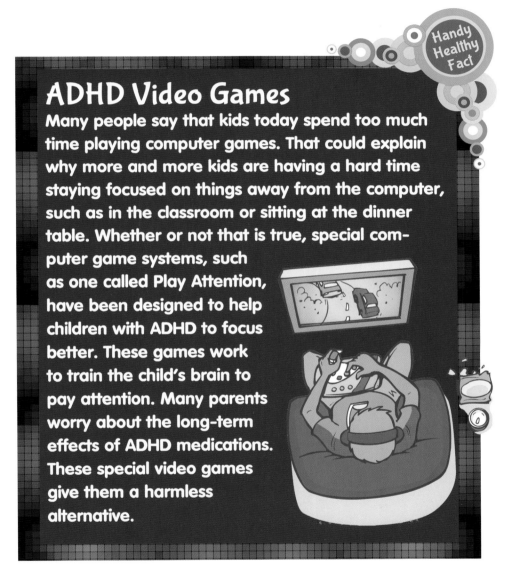

Discipline is also important. Kids with ADHD need to know that there are consequences for their behaviors. The child should be told what kind of behavior is not acceptable. If the child does not follow these rules, he or she should be taken to a quiet area to think about the situation. The parent should keep an eye on the child and not talk to him or her until the time is up.

It is very important for parents and teachers to have a lot of patience and understanding. Friends and family members can help too. Treatment can be a long, frustrating process, but kids with ADHD usually try hard to get better.

# 7

# WHAT YOU CAN DO

If you have ADHD, you are probably tired of hearing, "Why can't you sit still?" "Are you listening to me?" or "Did you forget your homework again?" You don't mean to get in trouble. By now, you know that it's not your fault that you act the way you do. Hopefully, you are getting help for your condition. Here is a list of some other things you can do to help yourself listen better, remember things better, and get things done.

- Write a note to yourself. Colored sticky notes are great because you can stick them anywhere.

TO DO LIST

- If your mom or dad wants you to do something, tell them to write you a note so you won't forget.
- Use a calendar to keep track of places you have to go.
- Try to do tasks right away. If you put them off for later, you might forget about them.
- If you have to go somewhere at a certain time, set the kitchen timer. For instance, if you have to go to soccer practice in a half hour, set the timer for 30 minutes.
- When you finish your homework, always put your schoolbooks in the same special place so that you won't have to hunt for them in the morning.
- Before you go to bed, decide what clothes you will be wearing the next day. That way you won't have to rush around in the morning.

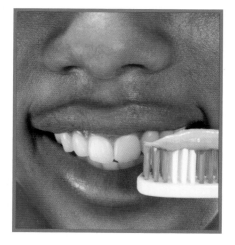

A morning routine that includes brushing your teeth and eating a healthful breakfast can help you get a good start to your day.

- Develop a morning routine: go to the bathroom, brush your teeth, take a shower, get dressed, eat breakfast, get your books, and go to school.

Many people with ADHD have found success with medication and behavior therapy. With a good treatment program and the support of their school, family, and friends, people with ADHD can finally have control over their lives.

Handy Healthy Fact

## Activity 2: Set Your Own Goals

If you have ADHD, make a list of five things that you want to do today. You may want to include doing your homework, cleaning up your room, giving your dog a bath, setting the table for dinner, or other daily chores. Write down how long each activity should take. Put a checkmark next to each item after you do it. At the end of the day, look at how many things you got done. How did you do? Each goal that you meet should make you feel proud of yourself. If you find you're having trouble getting things done, maybe you should make a new list every day and keep trying. Eventually, you'll be able to reach all your goals.

# GLOSSARY

**attention deficit hyperactivity disorder (ADHD)**—A condition characterized by an inability to concentrate, pay attention, and/or control one's actions.

**behavior modification**—A treatment often used to change behavior in people with ADHD.

**cerebral cortex**—The outermost layer of the brain. We use it to think, remember, make decisions, and control the movements of the body.

**combined type**—A kind of ADHD in which a person shows both inattentive and hyperactive-impulsive symptoms.

**diagnosis**—The identification of a medical condition from its symptoms.

**distracted**—Having trouble focusing attention on one thing for long.

**dopamine**—A neurotransmitter chemical that works in the brain to help focus attention.

**frontal lobe**—The part of the brain that helps you concentrate, make plans, and think before you act.

**genes**—Body chemicals that carry information about a person's characteristics.

**hyperactive-impulsive type**—A kind of ADHD. A hyperactive person has more energy than most people. An impulsive person acts without thinking.

**hyperactivity**—Having more energy than normal.

**impulse**—A sudden, unexplained action.

**inattentive type**—A kind of ADHD in which a person has difficulty paying attention; often called ADD (attention deficit disorder).

**inherited**—Passed on by genes from parents to children.

**neurotransmitter**—A chemical that carries messages from one part of the brain to another.

**overdiagnose**—To identify a certain illness more often than it actually occurs.

**Ritalin®**—A drug used to treat ADHD, especially the hyperactive type.

**self-esteem**—How you feel about yourself.

**stimulant**—A drug that can make most people feel more alert and energetic.

# LEARN MORE

## Books

Capccio, George. *ADD and ADHD*. New York: Marshall Cavendish Benchmark, 2008.

Chilman-Blair, Kim, and John Taddeo. *Medikidz Explain ADHD*. New York: Rosen Central, 2010.

Petersen, Christine. *Does Everyone Have ADHD: A Teen's Guide to Diagnosis and Treatment.* New York: Franklin Watts, 2006.

Taylor, John F. *The Survival Guide for Kids with ADD or ADHD*. Minneapolis, Minn.: Free Spirit Publishing, Inc., 2006.

Quinn, Patricia O., and Judith M. Stern. *Putting on the Brakes: Understanding and Taking Control of Your ADD or ADHD*. Washington, D.C.: Imagination Press, 2009.

## Web Sites

Children and Adults with Attention-Deficit/
    Hyperactivity Disorder (CHADD)
    <http://www.chadd.org>

The Nemours Foundation: TeensHealth.
    <http://kidshealth.org/Search01.jsp>

# INDEX